Gray
Whales

Other titles in the Returning Wildlife series include:

Returning Wildlife

Gray Whales

John E. Becker

KIDHAVEN PRESS

An imprint of Thomson Gale, a part of The Thomson Corporation

THOMSON

GALE

Detroit • New York • San Francisco • San Diego • New Haven, Conn.
Waterville, Maine • London • Munich

To my uncle Jess for his love of the natural world.

LIBRARY OF CONGRESS CATALOGING-IN-PUBLICATION DATA

Becker, John E., 1942–
   Gray Whales / by John E. Becker.
     p. cm. — (Returning wildlife)
   Includes index.
Summary: Discusses the history, characteristics, behavior, and habitat of gray whales including population decline and recovery and conservation efforts.
   ISBN 0-7377-2293-2
  1. Eschrichtiidae—Juvenile literature. I. Title. II. Series.
   QL737.C425B42 2005
   599.522—dc22
                                          2004002669

Printed in the United States of America

Contents

chapter 1

Gigantic Creatures

Gray whales were once plentiful in the waters along the Pacific and Atlantic coasts of North America. Though native hunters killed gray whales for food and oil, whale populations did not suffer until European whalers came to the New World in the 1500s. Within two hundred years, gray whales along the Atlantic coast had vanished.

About a hundred years after that, gray whales on the Pacific coast also began to disappear. By the end of the 1800s, gray whales were believed to be extinct.

This proved not to be the case. In the early 1900s, gray whales were discovered near the Pacific coast of North America. Whalers resumed their hunt, nearly wiping out the world's last known gray whales. Laws passed later in the century stopped this near disaster. Since that time, gray whales have increased in numbers. Today, gray whales along the Pacific coast of North America number approximately what they did before whaling began to threaten their existence centuries ago.

Ancient Species

The earliest ancestors of whales lived on land more than 50 million years ago. Those animals slowly adapted to living in the sea. They became the whales we know today. Whales are the largest creatures ever to live on Earth. Gray whales first appeared between 50,000 and 120,000 years ago. For as long as people have traveled the seas, they have been in awe of these gigantic creatures.

For many centuries, people believed that whales were a type of fish. In 1693, scientist John Ray established that whales are mammals. All whales are classified in the scientific order *Cetacea*, which comes from the Greek word for *sea monster.* Gray whales, especially mothers protecting their **calves,** were considered extremely aggressive. Sailors who hunted whales gave grays the nickname "devil fish" for that reason.

Huge Sea Mammals

Gray whales are slate gray in color with numerous white spots and blotches. Some of the spotting comes from **barnacles** that attach themselves to young gray whales and grow as the whale grows. Whale lice **parasites** (which look like tiny crabs) also live on the skin of gray whales. Some gray whales have been known to carry several

Gray whales are gigantic creatures. An adult whale can weigh up to forty tons.

hundred pounds of these creatures. The skin of a gray whale is smooth. It feels like a hard-boiled egg without the shell. Beneath the skin, whales have a thick layer of fat known as blubber. Blubber allows gray whales to stay warm in the icy-cold waters of the Arctic Ocean and stay cool in the warm waters of Baja California.

A full-grown gray whale is about half the size of the world's largest whale, the blue whale. The gray whale is about twice the size of a killer whale. Adult gray whales may be between 40 and 50 feet (12.2 to 15.2 meters) long (more than the length of a school bus). Female gray whales are slightly larger than males. Gray whales can weigh between 30 and 40 tons (27.2 and 36.3 metric tons) (twice the weight of an empty school bus).

Whales are divided into two groups—toothed whales and **baleen** whales. Gray whales are a type of baleen whale. Instead of teeth, gray whales have a series of long plates of hairlike mats that hang from their upper jaws. These baleen plates filter small fish and tiny shrimplike creatures from the mud on the ocean floor. Gray whales can stay underwater to feed for up to fifteen minutes, but they normally stay submerged for three to five minutes at a time. They feed mostly during the summer months of extended daylight hours in the cold waters between Alaska and Russia. A gray whale may go weeks or months without eating while traveling. But when they do feed, gray whales may consume up to a ton (0.9 metric tons) of food each day.

Excellent Swimmers

The gray whale is built to move quickly through the water. It has a **streamlined** body and a tapered head. It uses its large tail fluke, which may be from 10 to 12 feet (3 to 3.6 meters) across, to propel itself through the

Whale Sizes

An adult gray whale may be up to 50 feet in length, twice as large as the killer whale and half the size of the blue whale.

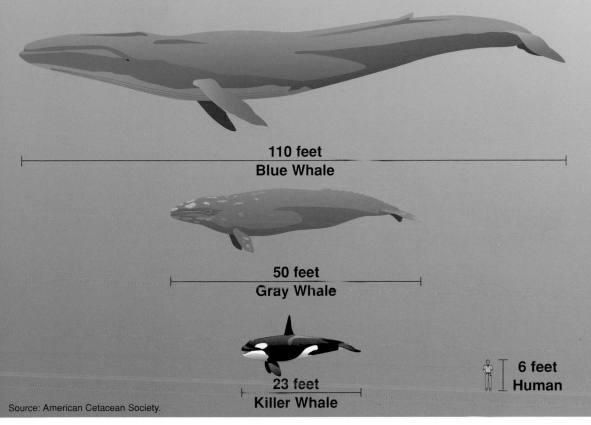

110 feet
Blue Whale

50 feet
Gray Whale

23 feet
Killer Whale

6 feet
Human

Source: American Cetacean Society.

water. When swimming at a leisurely pace, a gray whale will usually swim from 3 to 6 miles per hour (4.8 to 9.6 kilometers per hour). While being pursued, however, gray whales have been known to swim as fast as 10 to 12 miles per hour (16 to 19.3 kilometers per hour).

Whales are known for their spectacular leaps out of the water. This behavior is known as **breaching.** While breaching, a gray whale may leap out of the water with its nose as much as 30 feet (9.1 meters) in the air but with its tail still in the water.

Gray whales **migrate** each year to feed in the cold waters of the north. Then they migrate south again to breed

9

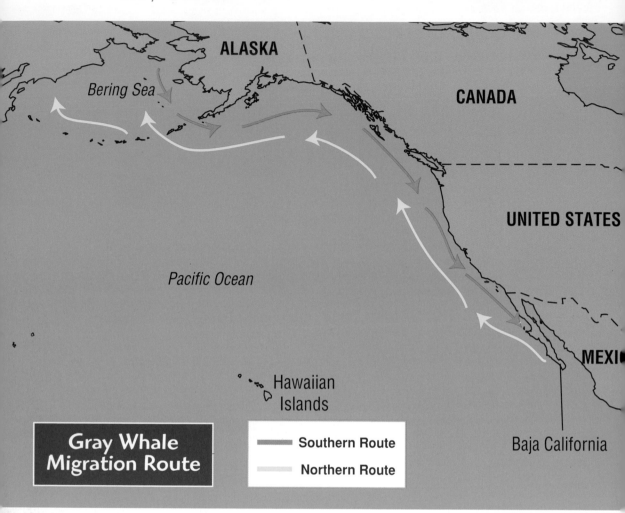

ALASKA

Bering Sea

CANADA

UNITED STATES

Pacific Ocean

MEXIC

Hawaiian
Islands

Baja California

**Gray Whale
Migration Route**

Southern Route
Northern Route

and give birth to their young in warm southern waters. They keep close to the shore for most of their long migration. They travel from the coasts of Alaska and Russia along the North American coast to Baja California and back again. Gray whales may cover between 10,000 and 14,000 miles (16,093 and 22,530 kilometers), which represents one of the longest migrations of any mammal on Earth.

Other Behaviors

Gray whales have good eyesight both in and out of the water. Some experts believe that having good vision helps them **navigate** on their long migrations. That has yet to be proven, however. A behavior known as spy hopping may give gray whales another way to observe the world around them. When spy hopping, a gray whale extends its head straight out of the water and holds itself in that position while treading water with its tail fluke.

Gray whales have good eyesight which may help them navigate during migration.

Like all whales, gray whales use **sonar** (sound waves they send out that bounce back from objects in the water). Sonar helps them find their way in the vast Pacific Ocean. Gray whales make a wide variety of sounds. Some of those sounds include groans, grunts, whistles, clicks, and rumbles. Scientists are not sure what each sound means. They are studying gray whale sounds in the hopes of learning more about how whales communicate with each other.

Gray whales also have a well-developed sense of hearing, which is quite useful in a dark ocean environment. A good sense of hearing allows them to hear other whales underwater.

Gray whales gather when they breed or when calves are being raised, but they do not normally travel or live together. Even though gray whales are not considered very sociable, they have been observed helping each other. This has led scientists to conclude that whales are intelligent animals. Gray whales have been seen lifting an injured whale's head out of the water so it can breathe. Two female gray whales were also observed nudging a calf free from a sandbar on which the calf had been stranded in a breeding **lagoon** in Baja California.

Breeding and Offspring

Gray whales reach breeding age anywhere from five to eleven years of age. Most gray whale breeding occurs after the whales have made the long migration from Alaska to Baja California. Breeding usually takes place in one of the sheltered lagoons along the coast of Baja. One or more males will mate with a female during the winter breeding season. Pregnant females return to the same warm water lagoons of Baja to give birth twelve to thirteen months after the pregnancy begins. Females

A swimming pair of gray whales is a common sight in San Ignacio Lagoon.

generally give birth every two to three years after they reach breeding age.

Mother gray whales will produce a single calf weighing between 1,100 and 1,500 pounds (498.9 and 680.3 kilograms). Newborn calves are dark gray with white markings and may be as long as 15 feet (4.6 meters) in

13

Gray whales usually breed along the coast of Baja.

length. Scientists are not sure how long gray whales live, but they believe that they live long lives, possibly as much as seventy years.

Gray whales have lived on earth for many centuries since adapting to an ocean environment. But during the 1800s and 1900s, they faced many challenges in their struggle to survive as a species.

chapter 2

Whaling Almost Leads to Extinction

The greatest natural predators of gray whales are killer whales. Adult gray whales are usually not at risk because of their large size, but gray whale calves are frequently attacked by killer whales and often killed. Natural predators, therefore, have always played a role in controlling gray whale populations.

Gray Whales Hunted for Centuries

Ancient Americans began hunting whales, including gray whales, at least nine thousand years ago. Native hunters killed whales for their baleen, oil, meat, and bone. Because Native Americans had only small boats and crude harpoons, their hunting probably did not hurt gray whale populations.

Gray whales only began disappearing from the Atlantic coast of North America after Europeans arrived in the 1500s. By that time, gray whales had disappeared from the Atlantic coast of Europe. European whalers pursued their prey to the northeast coast of North America. By the middle of the 1500s, more than forty whaling stations operated along the coast of Canada.

Whalers sailing out from those stations killed enough whales to produce 500,000 gallons (1.9 million liters) of whale oil. The oil was shipped back to Europe, where it lighted lamps in town centers and homes. The oil brought a handsome price. Owners of whaling ships often earned large profits on their investment.

Dutch whalers find ample prey in this engraving by a seventeenth-century artist.

Many countries sent whaling fleets to the New World to take part in the rich harvest of whales. Commercial whaling off the coast of what is now the United States began with the Dutch in 1632. In 1707, more than two hundred gray whales were killed off the coast of Long Island in New York. The species disappeared completely from the Atlantic Ocean by about 1750.

Along the Pacific Coast

When whales became scarce in the Atlantic Ocean, whalers began to search along the Pacific coast of South America. In 1789, the whaling ship *Emilia* sailed around the tip of South America into the Pacific Ocean. There the *Emilia* found many whales. Reports from the *Emilia* brought other whaling ships. An English whaling ship traveled to the southern tip of Baja California, for example, in 1793.

Over the next forty years, whaling ships from many countries arrived in the waters along the Pacific coast of North America. They began to take a heavy toll on gray whales. Thirty-two gray whales were killed in Magdalena Bay on the west coast of Baja California in 1845. More whalers followed. Between 1845 and 1848, approximately five hundred more gray whales were slaughtered in Magdalena Bay. The greatest wintering ground for gray whales had yet to be discovered, however.

Charles Melville Scammon

In 1849 Captain Charles Melville Scammon left New England for the Pacific coast of California. He participated in his first gray whale hunt in Magdalena Bay in 1853. Two years later his whaling ship, the *Leonore*, sailed into Jack Rabbit Spring Lagoon (later renamed Scammon's Lagoon). He discovered hundreds of gray whales basking in the warm-water lagoon off the Baja Peninsula. His crew killed twenty gray whales and took home five hundred barrels of whale oil. Scammon later returned to the lagoon, bringing six other whaling vessels with him.

Whalers from as far away as Russia and France came to the Baja Peninsula to share in the bounty of whale oil. In just a few years, over one thousand gray whales were killed in Scammon's Lagoon. When the whales of the lagoon became scarce, the whalers searched elsewhere. At Magdalena Bay, they killed more than fifteen hundred gray whales between 1854 and 1865.

The Business of Whaling

Whaling along the Pacific coast of North America became a huge business during the latter half of the 1800s. Gray whales' baleen, known as whalebone, was used in the making of corsets, fishing rods, buggy whips, umbrellas, skirt hoops, carriage springs, and furniture. Whale oil was also in great demand. It could be used as a fuel for home lighting and street lighting, as a lubricant in factories, and in the making of soap and paint. Each adult gray whale produced twenty-five to forty-five barrels of oil. Whale oil sold for twenty-seven dollars to forty-five dollars per barrel, making whaling very profitable in the 1800s. During the height of the Pacific whaling industry in the nineteenth century, over 650 ships and fifteen thousand men were employed in the business.

New deadly tools gave whalers an even greater advantage against their prey. An explosive, cannonlike harpoon gun fired from a swift, steam-powered ship meant many more kills in much less time. Whales stood little chance of surviving these methods. Almost eleven thousand gray whales were killed in the Pacific between

A nineteenth-century print shows wharf workers counting and measuring barrels of whale oil in preparation for shipment to Europe.

1846 and 1874. The slaughter had a disastrous effect. Many of those whales were females with calves. Breeding-age females and young gray whales were being wiped out. Experts believe that only about four thousand gray whales survived by the mid-1870s. Those whales were also hunted. By the end of the 1800s, gray whales were considered extinct.

Rediscovery

Once again, reports of gray whales' extinction came too soon. In 1912, **zoologist** Roy Chapman Andrews was visiting Japan when he heard that Japanese whalers were hunting nearby. He investigated and was shocked to see a whale that was thought to be extinct for thirty years—the gray whale. Andrews discovered that a population of gray whales was living in the waters near Asia.

A Japanese whaling gunner demonstrates a one-ton harpoon shooter used in modern-day whale hunting.

Those whales were being killed so rapidly, however, that Andrews believed they would become extinct before laws could be enacted for their protection. Within a few years of Andrews's discovery, gray whales were sighted once again off the coast of North America. The whale hunt began again and thousands of gray whales were slaughtered. Whaling reached its peak in the 1960s. In 1961 alone, whalers killed more than sixty-six thousand whales of all species. For the gray whale, the future seemed grim.

chapter 3

Gray Whales Come Back

The ocean is barely visible in the dull gray light of morning. Most residents of central California's coastal communities are still snuggled in their beds when biologists from the National Marine Fisheries Service (NMFS) arrive on a cliff overlooking the Pacific Ocean. The cliff, known as Granite Canyon, is one of the best viewing spots for the gray whales' southbound migration. Beginning in November, gray whales leave the cold waters off the coast of Alaska and head toward Baja California for the winter.

As the whales travel south, they stay close to the shoreline, which makes it easier for observers to count them. Spotters from the NMFS take up their positions on the Monterey Peninsula and all along the Pacific coast of North America to count the whales as they swim past. These counts provide a fairly accurate measure of gray whale populations.

Scientists and others have observed gray whale movements through this area during most seasons since 1967. Researchers now have enough information to be able to notice slight changes in patterns of gray whale behavior. Even minor changes in behavior may alert scientists to problems that could affect gray whales' ability to survive. Increased noise or boat traffic, for example, may cause gray whales to swim farther from shore. Keeping accurate counts of the whales also allows scientists to take steps early if gray whale populations drop.

Early Signs of Trouble

Scientists have been studying gray whales for centuries. English naturalist Paul Dudley made the first accurate scientific description of gray whales in 1725. Another 150 years would pass before a complete description of the physical characteristics and behaviors of gray whales would be published. Those descriptions were based on observations of whaler Charles Melville Scammon. His discovery of the primary gray whale breeding and **calving**

Because gray whales like to stay close to the shore, tourists are able to easily watch whales playing and swimming in the ocean.

lagoon in Baja California almost led to the extinction of gray whales. Later, however, Scammon became fascinated with the huge sea mammals. His keen observations would form the most complete record of gray whales for many years. They were published in 1874 in *The Marine Mammals of the Northwestern Coast of North America.* Scammon's book is still considered a classic work of natural history. By the time the book was published, gray whales

In a Washington, D.C., march, environmentalists protest Japanese whaling practices in the Antarctic in the 1980s.

were quite rare along the Pacific coast of North America. In his book, Scammon questioned whether gray whales would not soon be counted among the extinct species of the Pacific Ocean.

Scammon's prediction appeared to come true. Sightings of gray whales became increasingly rare over the next thirty to forty years. Some concerned people pushed for laws to protect whales, including gray whales. It would be many years before those laws would be passed.

Attempts to Protect Whales

The first real effort to protect whales came in 1931. Twenty-six countries signed an agreement to give whales legal protection. That agreement was called the Geneva Convention for the Regulation of Whaling. It was the first international law aimed at preventing the extinction of most species of whales. Because several whaling countries tried to block the adoption of the law, it did not go into effect until 1935. Even then Japan, Germany, and the Soviet Union refused to sign the agreement. Without the cooperation of those countries, the law had little effect.

In 1937, another attempt was made to provide protection for whales. The International Agreement for the Regulation of Whaling clearly stated that gray whales should not be killed. Once again, several countries refused to cooperate. Whale hunting continued. In just two years, between 1937 and 1938, fifty-five thousand whales of all species were killed. Many species of whales were in grave danger and may not have survived had war not broken out in Europe in 1939.

During World War II, most whaling vessels were converted to oil transports for the war effort. Whaling halted, and gray whale populations increased. Once the war ended, whaling resumed. Whalers now had even more advanced equipment, such as former warplanes and helicopters, to spot whales at sea.

One more try at getting international cooperation on a whaling ban failed. In 1946, the International Whaling Commission (IWC) was formed in Washington, D.C. As with earlier efforts, the Soviet Union, Japan, and other whaling countries refused to cooperate. During IWC's first thirty years, over 1.5 million whales were killed around the world.

Real Protection

Nothing much changed until the 1970s. Mexico took the first big step in 1972. The government passed a law to protect gray whale breeding and calving lagoons in Baja California. That same year, the United Nations called for the end of whaling worldwide, and the United States passed the Marine Mammal Protection Act. This act makes it illegal to import or kill whales and other marine mammals. The United States also passed the Endangered Species Act in 1973. Under this act, gray whales were listed as endangered animals within U.S. waters, making it illegal to harass, capture, or kill gray whales. The NMFS is charged with the responsibility of keeping track of gray whale populations to ensure that action can be taken if they begin to decline once again. Canada also passed laws protecting whales. These included the Cetacean Protection Regulations in 1982. Because gray whales are protected in the United States, Mexico, and Canada, they can now migrate freely.

With legal protections in place, gray whales began making a rapid recovery. By 1975, scientists estimated that gray whale populations had increased to more than ten

Sea World Animal Rescue and Rehabilitation personnel release a gray whale into the ocean. Whales receive help from many different organizations.

thousand. There were so many gray whales now that IWC felt that it could safely allow limited hunting of them.

Whales have also received a great deal of help from private conservation organizations. In 1969, the conservation organization Greenpeace was formed in Canada, and it quickly became a strong voice for the preservation of whales. "Save the Whale" became a rallying cry for Greenpeace to attract the attention of people around the

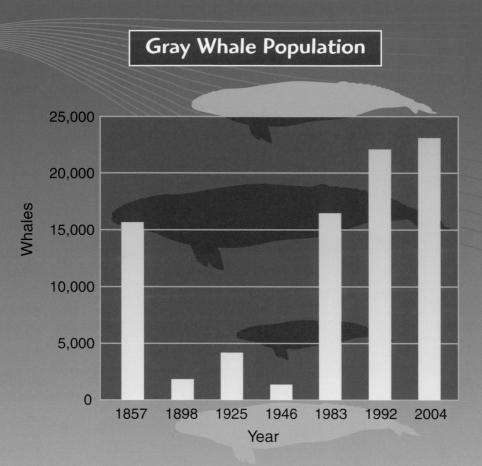

Gray Whale Population

Source: San Luis Obispo County Office of Education.

world to the plight of whales. The public outcry over the slaughter of whales helped stop most whaling.

An Amazing Recovery

Gray whales continued their recovery through the 1980s. By 1983, gray whale populations were estimated at more than fifteen thousand. By 1994, the gray whales' comeback was complete. In that year, they became the first marine mammal ever to be removed from the Endangered Species List.

Gray Whale Recovery a Conservation Triumph

Today, gray whale recovery is considered a major conservation success story. Having recovered from near extinction twice is reason for celebration. Gray whales have now almost returned to the numbers that existed before whaling came close to wiping them out in the 1800s. The species has excellent prospects for the future, but some serious threats remain.

chapter 4

The Future for Gray Whales

The streamlined hull of the large boat cut swiftly through the blue waters of the Pacific Ocean off Southern California. Next to the boat, a large pod of dolphins playfully kept pace.

Just ahead, a huge form rose to the surface of the water. The twin spouts of watery mist rising into the air helped to identify the creature as a gray whale.

The sight of the enormous animal brought oohs and aahs from the passengers crowded along the boat railing. As the gray whale swam on the surface for several hundred yards, the people on the deck of the **whale watching** boat took photos and video of the exciting scene.

When the whale left the surface for a dive, it rose in the surf momentarily and then plunged beneath the waves. The whale's large tail fluke shot into the air at the peak of the dive.

All along the Pacific coast of North America, boats filled with eager spectators are setting off in pursuit of whales. Whale watching began as a business in California during the 1950s. Today, more than fifty companies and nonprofit organizations offer whale watching opportunities in California. Whale watching tours are available along a great deal of the seacoast of the United States. More than forty countries also promote whale watching tours. Whale watching is a major worldwide industry providing local people with money from tourism and giving tourists educational information about whales and other marine life. Whale watching also provides scientific data for studies of gray whales. While there are many advantages to increased human interest in whales, there are also a number of problems associated with people interacting with whales.

Threats Remain

Each year more people attempt to view whales from boats. Many whale watching boats take precautions to avoid causing stress to the whales, but some boaters

Tourists reach out to touch the head of a gray whale. Whale watching tours have become very popular.

approach too close or create confusion that can be harmful to the whales. In some instances, boaters have been observed harassing whales by chasing them.

Greater ship traffic in gray whale migration routes results in more collisions between ships and whales. The number of serious injuries and deaths from ship collisions has increased over the past several years. Increased commercial shipping traffic and recreational

Boaters who get too close to gray whales can create stress and confusion for the whales.

boating along the Pacific coast of North America also forces gray whales farther from shore. The increased water depth makes food more difficult to find.

Another threat is the increased danger of attack from pods of killer whales on mothers and their young as they migrate from the Baja California lagoons to Alaska during their northerly migration. The closer gray whale mothers and their calves can travel to the shore-line, the greater protection they have from killer whale attacks. Killer whales are more likely to attack from deeper water, so gray whale mothers keep their calves between themselves and the shore.

Because gray whales depend on their sonar abilities for communication, some scientists believe that the sounds from oil drilling may cause them to become confused. Confusion from oil drilling sounds could lead to gray whales losing contact with each other, including mothers from their babies. The oil drilling sounds may also cause gray whales to avoid areas with a good supply of the small shrimplike animals they depend upon for food. Other factors may also cause prey animals to disappear.

Pollution poses another threat to gray whales. The exact effect of pollution on gray whales and their prey has yet to be determined. Some scientists believe that pollution has already lowered the number of prey animals that are available to gray whales.

Projects to Ensure Future Health of Gray Whale Populations

Between 1999 and 2000, over three hundred gray whales mysteriously died and washed ashore between Mexico and Alaska. Scientists do not know the cause of the die-off. They have ruled out disease. One guess is that gray whale populations have now exceeded the food supply and that some of the gray whales are dying of starvation. Some scientists believe that gray whales and their prey animals are being harmed by human activities and that the gray whales' prey animals have been reduced.

Gray whales feed extensively in the Bering Sea and the Chukchi Sea between Alaska and Russia. One study has suggested that the food supply has, indeed, declined in that region. It has been suggested that changing ocean temperatures, possibly as a result of **global warming** (a gradual increase in the temperature of the earth's atmosphere), may be responsible for the loss of prey animals. Some prey animals may only be able to survive in cooler waters, and if the water temperature increases, those animals will die.

Stopping a Threat

Concerned people stopped at least one project that might have harmed gray whales. In 1995, the Mexican government and the Mitsubishi Company of Japan announced plans to develop the world's largest salt-producing plant at the San Ignacio Lagoon in Baja California. That lagoon is the last unspoiled breeding and calving sanctuary for gray whales. The plans for the salt plant called for the development of over five hundred thousand acres of the Vizcaino Desert Biosphere Reserve. This is Latin America's largest protected area.

The proposed salt plant would have included evaporation ponds, pumping stations, and a mile-long dock for oceangoing ships that would have interfered with gray whales trying to reach their breeding lagoons. Water would have been pumped out of the lagoon at the rate of almost seven thousand gallons per second. After the evaporation process, a poisonous brine solu-

A dead gray whale lies on a beach in Alaska after the *Exxon Valdez* oil spill in 1989.

tion would be left over. That brine would have been dangerous to gray whales and other aquatic plants and animals if the solution had leaked back into the lagoon. The salt plant would not only have harmed gray whales, it also would have harmed many other plants and animals, including pronghorn antelope, green sea turtles, dolphins, sea lions, and many wild bird species.

An environmental organization in Mexico, The Group of 100, protested the proposed salt plant. It contacted

Every winter whales migrate from the north to the warm, protected waters of San Ignacio Lagoon in Baja, California, to breed and nurse their young.

people in the United States and around the world for help. Millions of people, including many children, wrote letters in support of The Group of 100. Several conservation organizations also joined the fight to stop the building of the proposed salt plant. The pressure brought to bear by the worldwide protest paid off in 2000. In that year, the president of Mexico announced that plans to build the salt plant had been cancelled.

Learning More About Gray Whales

Students from across the United States, Mexico, and Canada are also showing their concern about the gray whale. In a program called Journey North, students participate in tracking activities for migrating species. The

Although gray whales still face many threats to their survival, their population is growing.

program includes almost 540,000 students in more than eleven thousand schools. Journey North improves children's math, reading, and science skills as they become "citizen scientists." The Journey North Web site provides extensive information about gray whales, their characteristics, life cycle, ecology, and conservation. Students help track the movements of gray whales along the Pacific coast of North America each spring, learning important information about gray whales.

Continued Growth in Numbers

The current population estimate for gray whales is between nineteen thousand and twenty-three thousand in the waters along the Pacific coast of North America. That marks a major conservation success for a species of marine mammal once thought to be extinct. Gray whales still face threats to their survival, however, and people must help eliminate those threats in the future.

baleen: Fringed, platelike sheets that hang from the upper jaws of nontoothed whales and are used to filter small sea animals for food.

barnacles: Small shellfish that attach themselves to boats, whales, and other shellfish.

breaching: A spectacular display in which the whale comes almost completely out of the water and crashes back into the water.

calves: The young of whales.

calving: Giving birth to a newborn whale.

global warming: A gradual increase in the temperature of the earth's atmosphere caused by gases such as carbon dioxide collecting in the atmosphere and preventing the sun's heat from escaping.

lagoon: A shallow lake located close to the shore that joins a larger body of water.

migrate: To travel from one place to another and back again, usually at times of seasonal changes.

navigate: To travel on or over the land or water while controlling one's course.

parasite: An animal or plant that gets its food from another plant or animal that it lives on or inside.

sonar: A guidance system in which sound waves are sent out and bounce off other objects and then back to the sender.

streamlined: Shaped to move through the air or water quickly.

whale watching: Commercial tours focused on observations of whales in their natural environment.

zoologist: A person who studies animals.

Books

Caroline Arnold and Richard Hewett, *Baby Whale Rescue: The True Story of J.J.* Mahwah, NJ: Bridgewater Books, 1999. True story of the rescue, rehabilitation, and release of the gray whale J.J. by the staff of Sea World of California.

Jim Darling, *Gray Whales.* Grantown-on-Spey, Scotland: Colin Baxter Photography, 1999. Gives the natural history of gray whales from the perspective of their incredible migration up and down the Pacific coast of North America.

Francois Gohier, *A Pod of Gray Whales.* Parsippany, NJ: Silver Burdett Press, 1995. Presents the life history of gray whales with extensive information about the species' five-thousand-mile migration from Alaska to Baja California and back each year.

John Klobas, *Life Cycle of the Pacific Gray Whale.* Torrance, CA: Heian International, 1993. Story of the life cycle of a Pacific gray whale from birth through adulthood.

Bernard Stonehouse, *A Visual Introduction to Whales, Dolphins, and Porpoises.* New York: Checkmark Books, 1998. An introduction for children to the cetaceans of the world through beautiful illustrations and easy-to-understand text.

Periodicals

Michelle R. Derrow, "A Warm Welcome in Mexico's Lagoons: Homero Aridjis Works to Preserve the Gray Whales' Winter Home," *Time for Kids,* January 15, 2000. The story of the efforts of the Mexican conservation organization, The Group of 100, to prevent the Mexican government and the Mitsubishi Company from building the world's largest salt plant on San Ignacio Lagoon, which is one of the primary breeding and calving lagoons for gray whales.

Time for Kids, "A Whale of a Tale: A Gray Whale Raised at Sea World Must Learn to Live in the Sea," March 13, 1998. Relates the story of J.J., a newborn gray whale calf that washed ashore, was rescued by people, raised at Sea World of California, and released back into the ocean.

Organizations to Contact

American Cetacean Society
PO Box 1391
San Pedro, CA 90733-1391
(310) 548-6279
www.acsonline.org

The world's oldest whale conservation organization, which has worked to protect whales, dolphins, porpoises, and their habitats since 1967 through education, conservation, and research.

National Marine Fisheries Service
Southwest Regional Office
501 W. Ocean Blvd.
Long Beach, CA 90802-4213
(562) 980-4000
http://swr.nmfs.noaa.gov

The government agency charged with the responsibility for maintaining living marine resources and healthy ecosystems through science-based conservation and management.

The Ocean Conservancy
1725 DeSales St.
Suite 600
Washington, DC 20036
(202) 429-5609
www.oceanconservancy.org
Utilizing advocacy, research, and education, this private organization works to conserve and restore ocean ecosystems and the marine life associated with the world's oceans.

Web Site

Journey North (www.learner.org). Private conservation and education organization focused on providing children with opportunities to observe migrating species of wildlife, thus improving their math, reading, and science skills.

Video

The Undersea World of Jacques Cousteau—the Desert Whales. Pacific Arts Video, 1989. Jacques Cousteau and the crew of the *Calypso* follow gray whales to their breeding grounds in the sheltered lagoons of Baja California. Many facts about gray whales, their reproductive behavior, and their lengthy migrations are shared, including an attempted rescue of a stranded baby whale.

Special Thanks To:

Joe Cordaro, National Marine Fisheries Service
Jane Duden, Journey North
Gordon Helms, National Marine Fisheries Service
Morgan S. Lynn, National Marine Fisheries Service
Jim Milbury, National Marine Fisheries Service
Wayne Perryman, National Marine Fisheries Service
David J. Rugh, National Marine Fisheries Service
Brent Stewart, Hubbs Sea World
James Sumich, Grossmont College

Acknowledgements

John E. Becker writes books and magazine articles about nature and wild animals for children. He graduated from Ohio State University in the field of education. He has been an elementary school teacher, college professor, and zoo administrator and has worked in the field of wildlife conservation with the International Society for Endangered Cats. He currently lives in Delaware, Ohio, and teaches writing at the Thurber Writing Academy. He also enjoys visiting schools and sharing his love of writing with kids. In his spare time, Becker likes to read, hike in the woods, ice skate, and play tennis.